*"Birth the Treasure Within"*

*"Birth the Treasure Within"*
*Believe in You*
*Believe in Your Greatness*
*Empower Yourself*

Copyright © 2009 by Karen L. Ross
*"Birth the Treasure Within"*
Written and published by Karen L. Ross
*Editing – Carole Harmon*
*Printed in the United States of America*

# INTRODUCTION

*T*he title of this book comes from realizing and believing there are treasures in each and every one of us. We have great power instilled in us from the beginning. It is in you, it is in me. I believe we are created with and for greatness. For whatever reason, that treasure within is buried, dormant, suppressed waiting to be birthed. Waiting to be revealed and used, not only for self but also for humanity. We have the ability to be prosperous and successful in every area of our lives; spiritually, physically, emotionally, relationally, economically and mentally. The "University of Life" recruits us and we allow situations and circumstances to keep us from graduating into our true potential – our true self – that person we are created to be. I say dig and believe there is great potential within. Dig deep and **"Birth Your Treasure Within."**

In doing so believe and **"trust the process."**

**What is your treasure?**

Use this book as your personal journal, workbook and/or guide. Every empty space is your pallet for your thoughts and creativity. **Use it to your advantage!**

# DEDICATION

*I* dedicate this book to the various flowers who have inspired me at various stages of my life. They have represented beauty, strength and spirit. My grandmother – Fannie Ray-Jacobs, my mother – Celia Theodosia Jacobs – Ross, my aunt – Ivory Jane Cozart and Vanessa Goodwyn.

*A flower so delicate, it opens to reveal life. Life to display beauty, essence, character. Nourished by the spirit of the earth. Nourishment so plentiful and taking only what it needs to survive, to become this essence of beauty. To unlock the aroma of such process with no thought. Just is. The rays of the sun provide, warmth, essential elements to become strong but yet so delicate. Symbolic of love. Love for sight, smell, touch and thought. An example of creation.. Powerful. Imagine a field of love, unlimited. Smell the power of creation. See the beauty within. Display your beauty. The field is waiting.*

Thank you for your beauty and allowing it to illuminate. You have revealed love and strength, which inspires me to move forward and birth the treasure within me.

*I hope this book inspires you to believe in the greatness inside you.*

*The creativity, the gifts, the talents and skills you possess.*

*No matter where you are at this moment you can change.*

*You are greater than what you have been told and the belief system you have adopted.*

*Begin your journey to a new and better you.*

*"Birth Your Treasure Within"*

## "THE MIRROR"

*e live in this world and we see opportunities for change. We want a better world but that better world starts with me and it starts with you. For the world to change it would require action from each individual. It would require evaluating, acknowledgment and the willingness to change. It would take looking at our contribution to the space, the community, the society the world we occupy.*

### Self-Evaluation:

*How often do I look in the mirror?*

*How often do I look within to take self-inventory of MY beliefs, attitudes and behaviors?*

*What do I see?*

*Do I like what I see?*

*As we look in the mirror consider some of the questions and statements below:*

*My life has purpose and meaning. I am valuable to myself, my family and community. What strategies am I using to help me fulfill MY purpose?*

- ~ *Am I willing to change MY negative beliefs, negative attitude and negative behavior to fulfill MY purpose?*

- ~ *What I have received and learned in the past can be changed for the benefit of the future.*

- ~ *Am I more concerned about race (physical characteristics) or the human race (mankind)?*

- ~ *What am I willing to do to change MY negative and faulty beliefs, attitude and behavior to help make this world look and feel different?*

*It is never too late. No matter what age, what situation or circumstance, you can start today.*

*Today, at this moment, agree with yourself to be the person YOU are created to be and live the life YOU are created to live and make the difference YOU can make.*
*Imagine the possibilities, expand YOUR vision.*

*"The field is waiting".*

*If each individual would be willing to look at themselves in the mirror on a daily basis, evaluate, acknowledge and change the negative and faulty attitudes, values, beliefs and behaviors, the world would look and feel a lot different.*

# "WHO AM I?"

*Throughout our life we have taken on the personality and characteristics of others. We have become who others wanted us to be, doing what others wanted us to do. Now, here we are dealing with the regrets and disappointments of a life that we really did not want. When do we give up control of our lives to others to intimidate and manipulate us into being this stranger we are now living with? Not fulfilling a life we are purposed to fulfill. Some of us don't know who we are, what we want to do or where we want to go. In conversations I have had with some adults and youth, I have asked the question, "What would you like to do, what are your dreams, what is your passion?" Many answer, "I don't know." Give them a few minutes to think of the many possibilities and still the response is "I don't know". What are the dynamics that lead to the state of not knowing who or what we want to do with our own lives? We exist in a state of confusion. I say existing instead of living because I believe when you live life, you are taking advantage of the total you, your true potential, fulfilling your created purpose, taking advantage of the opportunities that life has to offer. We recognize and act upon the freedom to create opportunities that are life changing for the betterment of self and others - the glass ceiling is no longer restricting, and the box has no limits. Our minds are open and we can transition from the negatives that have kept us bound to the bountiful blessings awaiting us. If we look at where we are right now, can we honestly say who we are and what is occurring in our lives at this instant is the best that it can be? Many would probably say, "Oh, I am fine, I'm ok." If we think about it, are we really?*

*Are we fine with ok, or do we want excellence and expansion?*

*Can we honestly and sincerely believe in our heart and say 100% we are living fulfilled lives?*

*Are we living our true selves?*

*Take a quiet moment to go within and search **YOU**.*
*Be honest and true to yourself and answer the following questions. Evaluate every area of YOUR life.*

~ *"Who am **I**?"*

~ *Am **I** living to **my** truest potential?*
*If not, why and what do **I** need to change?*

~ *What do **I** believe about **myself**?*

~ *Where do **I** want to be?*

~ *What do **I** want to do?*

~ *What do **I** love to do?*

~ *What am **I** most passionate about?*

~ *What does LOVE mean to ME?*

~ *Do **I** LOVE **myself**? If no, why?*

*Any unwelcoming thought(s) or belief(s) I have of myself are no longer welcome. I will positively affirm myself everyday – morning, noon and night. I believe in my greatness and I refuse to let me or anyone else believe contrary about me. I look in the mirror and I see power, strength and beauty. I look past and beyond my self-defeating thoughts and conditions. I will be optimistic about my future and I look forward to being the best I am created to be. I will live to my truest potential to be my authentic self and will be honest and true to myself. I will love me like no other has loved me. I know my Creator loves me and thinks beyond the world of me.*

*"I AM A TREASURE!"*

# REFLECTIONS

*After answering the questions regarding you, another question would be, is my family, my community and others I am connected to, living fulfilled lives? Remember, in the long run it is not just about you or me.*

*Sincerely look at yourself, your relationships, your family and your community and ask:*

*Can I do more? If so, what?*

*What would I need to do to implement my project?*

*What resources do I need to seek for change to occur? Who do I need to contact? (Write down the process)*

*Knowing who we are and being true to ourselves is key to unlocking the treasure and living a fulfilling abundant life. I am not referring to just material and financial gain, I am referring to the type of life where fantasy of living becomes a reality. I have given up the dreams of living the life I read about; see on television and in the movies. I believe I have the potential to become the loving, confident, secure, strong enthusiastic, self-reliant individual I am created to be. I believe I deserve peace even in the midst of the chaos and confusion around me.*

*I believe the first six to eight years of a person's life are crucial. We are created to be individuals of unique character. Character to be used for the benefit of not just self, but for others as well. As stated earlier, the early years of a person's life are crucial. Development is taking place; personality and character are being formed. It is detrimental for the sake of the child and humanity that productive characteristics are fulfilled in early years. Whatever is established in a person's life in early years manifests itself in later years – positive or negative. Throughout our lives our character matures and there is growth. Love, nurturing and affirmations are only a few essential elements to creating and developing a loving, caring self-sufficient, altruistic human being. Finding out who we are and what we want to do creates the opportunity to living endless possibilities. The sky is no longer the limit when we know and believe in ourselves, the power within and what we are destined to become.*

*Commit to the time, energy and space to develop all the essential elements to discard the "I don't know" in your being. You are that valuable. As long as we don't know, that is who we become. Do not settle or compromise your self-worth and value on not knowing. We can evaluate why we don't know who, what, when, where and why. That is when time for self becomes crucial and why it is so important. The spiritual connection we have to our CREATOR is the number one tool to help us dig and reveal our treasure. The willingness, openness and honesty we provide ourselves as we go through the evaluation process will give us the freedom to capture the very things that are not a part of who we truly are and want to be.*

*We can find out so much when we spend quiet, quality time with ourselves. I say date yourself. Commit to self so self will know who, what, when, where and why.*

*Learn you. Journal as you go through the process. The end result can be blessings.*

*Life is more than the material possessions we accumulate and hoard. I realize the things we have around us we hold onto, we cherish them, we spend time with them, and we love them more than we love ourselves and others. We cut ourselves off and cheat ourselves from possessing the greatest investment and asset we can ever own – ourselves. We allow ourselves to lack the freedom, peace of mind, strength, confidence, love for self and love for others. Not the blueprint of life.*

*Am I my possessions?*

*Are my possessions and I one?*

*How would I feel if I were to lose my material possessions at this moment?*

*Am I mentally, emotionally, spiritually, physically and financially able to handle a loss?*

*Do I value my material possessions more than myself and others?*

*Do I seek money and material possessions more than I seek myself?*

*Does money and material possessions provide a sense of well being for me?*

*Do I put more time, money, energy and effort into the things around me than my health, my physical well-being, my spirituality?*

*How much time do I dedicate to immaterial things and others?*

*How much time do I dedicate to myself and seeking after that which is going to better me and add value to my life and the life of others?*

*Are my accomplishments based on things or the things I have or is it based on my integrity, my strength and faith?*

*What we possess inside of ourselves is more than what we possess outside of ourselves. You can replace your material possessions but can you replace your dignity, your integrity, your life?*

*If the opportunity presented itself to move forward in my purpose am I willing to give up my possessions? If no, why?*

# REFLECTIONS

# BIRTH

*A*lthough I have never experienced the birth of a child, I am experiencing the birth of a dream/vision. About 15 years ago I had the opportunity to be present during the birth of my cousin and witnessed the beauty of birthing life. To actually be present in the labor and delivery room, I thought, was one of the neatest and most exciting things. After the birth, tears of joy, tears of life flowed. The anticipation of finally getting to see and meet this new creation. To witness this miracle of life. It was an experience I will never forget. I remember being anxious, waiting for the arrival of a new creation. One never existing. one never seen before. How exciting. In the room there was a team of nurses and doctors, plus the equipment to be able to monitor and make the process go as smoothly as possible. And then there was the mother. The vessel used to nurture and care for this miracle that was about to emerge. Nine months bearing, expecting. Nine months of carrying life inside of her. Nine months of change. The time was here. It was happening and there was no turning back. Enduring the birthing process was inevitable. Forward was the only option.

This being my first time witnessing birth, I was anxious. Every time she would experience a contraction I would turn and watch the monitor. As I watched the monitor during the contractions I remember saying as the contractions became stronger, "Let's see how high they go this time." The monitor was approaching the 70's and continuing to rise. I said, "Let's see if it can get up to a 100." My cousin was not amused at the time. That was before she got the epidural. We laugh about it now.

When it was time everyone was in position doing what needed to be done; my cousin, her team of doctors and nurses, there to assist, to coach. Everyone experienced in his or her craft, in place, working jointly side-by-side together to achieve a common goal – **to birth life**, to birth this treasure, this valuable gift.

Well, for those who have a passion, a dream, a vision and so desperately want to give birth to them, we have been anxiously awaiting and anticipating your miracle. You have gone through months or even years of changes, pains, cravings, emotions, sleepless nights, etc., etc., etc. It is time. There is no looking back. It is time to move forward.

*At this point, ask yourself (Remember to be honest and true to you).*

*What would keep me from going through the process?*

*Is it fear? (Fear of failure, fear of the unknown, fear of embarrassment, fear of _____)*

*What is the worst that can happen? What is the worse that cannot happen? (Look at both sides)*

*Is it my concern what others think? Why is that a concern? Why am I placing more value on what others think, rather than my own beliefs about my value?*

*Do I have confidence in myself? If not, why?*

*Confidence is self-assurance arising from your appreciation of your own abilities or qualities. It is courage, it is boldness, and it is poise.*

*Be confident in your ability to birth your treasure within. Be bold and allow yourself the time and freedom to go through the process. Appreciate you. Love and appreciate who you are created to be – no matter what.*

Pain can be a deterrent especially when it is so excruciating we start to look for something or someone to relieve us. During the birthing process the choice to endure and go natural is an option, or the choice to receive an anesthetic that is introduced to produce loss of sensation below the waist is another. Whichever you choose there is going to be pain. The difference is tolerance. What comes to mind in birthing dreams is "FAITH." Faith in knowing that whatever was placed in you is beyond what you see, think or feel; but having the faith to know the one who created you, the one whose image is in you, the one who is molding and shaping you for greatness. Believing your CREATOR is there with you and is part of your team.

How strong and how high did your pain levels grow when you felt like there was about to be a breakthrough? During the process how tolerant were you? Did you feel like giving up? Did you give up? Are you asking yourself or wondering, "If I would have pushed a little harder, endured the pain a little longer I would have my anticipated miracle." How often do we want to give up because the pain is too severe or it is too difficult to endure? We look for something to numb the pain but at times it is too late, *out of reach or not available. We look to others to make a way; we call screaming – shouting for relief but to no avail. We still have to bear our own dream/vision. We may have had a team to help with the process but to no avail. They may not be qualified or may not be the right person to help bring forth what is so valuable. I know the experience is not the same and cannot compare, but I believe I can express my dream being birthed in addition to my birthing experience. Birth can be defined not only as the emergence of a human life, but the beginning or coming into existence of something. To birth the treasure within would be to bring into existence that which has been and continues to be buried in us for greatness. We are unique in our way. There is no one like you, there is no one like me. Only you can do what you were created to do. Until we recognize who we are and believe in our power and potential we deceive ourselves; robbing ourselves and others of the valuable, natural ability or talents that can make a difference not only in our personal life but the lives of others. Birth can be painful but once birth takes place there is joy like no other. Once your dream/vision has emerged you have brought into existence something beautiful and unique based on your personality and your characteristics. It has your print/seal on it. To go beyond the expectations and be the recipient of something life changing and beautiful just for you is an emotion identifiable only by you. To be given the responsibility and task to implement, develop, nurture and build a business can create anxiety as much as birthing a baby can create anxiety. If your dream is writing a book, singing, traveling – seeing the rest of the world, using your voice to inspire others, whatever it may be expand your mind, expand your vision. Because there are no guarantees and fear of an uncertain outcome can cause us not to take chances, we are self-defeating ourselves before we get started. We may question our ability of being a good father or mother or ask, "Do I have what it takes to be successful in starting and building a business?" We ride through life wondering and wandering. Wondering what if and wandering from place to place not fulfilled, knowing this is not where we want to be. But because of the self-defeating mindset we choose to stay complacent and continue to wonder and wander. We know there is something deep in us that we would be more fulfilled doing, but we allow fear to take over, the past to keep us from moving forward and we adopt the belief system, "I can't" to talk us out of who we are created to be. It is time to "change." It is time to open our closed minds. It is time to say, "No more will I allow wonder, wander and past to keep me from my fullest potential." We have expectations of what we want our lives to be like or look like. Expectations are strong beliefs that something will happen, someone will achieve something. Expectations without action are just expectations. Expectations coupled with action can create reality. Having a dream/vision and expecting them to come true takes energy of belief and an effort of strength from within to capitalize on the end result. It has been stated time and time again, fear is false evidence appearing real. We allow fear to grip us and bind us from capitalizing on so much of what we are created to experience. We believe great things, we dream great things, we talk about great things but again, dreaming, believing and talking is just that until you put action to it. You can have your dream car, a full tank of gas, key in the ignition, car on, sitting, idling. It is not until you put it in drive that you start moving towards your destination. You can have the expectation of getting to your destination. Excited about where you are going, dressed up and ready to go. Can you picture that? Imagine that for a moment. You are ready. People are awaiting your arrival. You are the catalyst for the event. The key person that can make a difference. You have everything you need but you are sitting, idling. Burning gas, burning time. It is costing you. It is cheating us.*

*Birth is a process that results in an overwhelming sense of joy. Yes, fear and anxiety are natural emotions. But so are disappointments. Joy or disappointment you decide. Start your birthing process. Choose to stop idling and start the process of birthing your treasure within.*

*We are waiting for your gift.*

*What is <u>MY</u> passion?*

*What do <u>I</u> love to do?*

*Who or what is keeping <u>ME</u> from giving birth to <u>my</u> treasure?*

*Why am <u>I</u> allowing who or what to keep <u>ME</u> from birthing <u>MY</u> treasure? (Remember choices)*

*Am <u>I</u> willing to endure the pain, no matter what? If no, why?*

*Do <u>I</u> believe <u>I</u> have value and am valuable?*

*What do <u>I</u> understand about faith?*

*Is <u>MY</u> hope and trust in people, things or the SPIRIT within <u>ME</u>?*
*Do <u>I</u> have more faith in what others can do for <u>ME</u> or do <u>I</u> have more faith in what <u>I</u> can do for <u>MYSELF</u>?*

*What belief system resides in <u>ME</u> keeping <u>ME</u> from believing <u>MY</u> greatness?*

# REFLECTIONS

## "TREASURE"

*There are times when I disengage myself from others, events and the outside world. I retreat for the comfort of working on myself, my issues and purpose. I believe my passion and I are that important. I find there are times when it is definitely needed. I find when I go through the process of "me" I am wiser and stronger because of it. There are days when it is challenging and difficult but I have found the reward is greater than the challenge. When you have a passion, a strong passion for being and living the person you are created to be, alone time is one of the most important things you can gift yourself. Especially when being and staying focused on the project/task at hand is essential. To go within and search myself helps me to know who KAREN is – her likes, her dislikes, knowing her boundaries. Evaluating and reevaluating asking questions. It becomes more and goes deeper than the outward appearance. It surpasses what others believe and think, because at the end of the day, at the end of my life I have to live with me. I have to know that what I have done, I have fulfilled and lived to my truest potential. So, quieting me, taking time* for me to think, dating me to get to know me is crucial. I am that VALUABLE. When we meet someone we are interested in we spend time with that person. In the beginning we want to spend as much time with that person as we possibly can. If we don't have time, we will make time. We are anxious about spending time with this new person in our lives. How about getting anxious about the person you are about to recreate in yourself? The gifts you are about to reveal, let's get anxious about that. When dating there are expectations, wants and desires. There is a process; stages towards a relationship if we really like them and find value, possibly a commitment. There is and should be a process to the end result. There are goals, there are plans, looking towards something more meaningful. We seek truth by asking questions, not necessarily always getting the truth, but we inquire. There is and should be effective communication – talking, listening, paying attention to body language, paying attention to actions not just words, listening to what is said or not said. We want to know this person and want to find out as much as we possibly can about them. This person is now occupying my space, my time and my energy. I am allowing this person to have access to me. At times we may go as far as *communicating with family members, friends, coworkers and neighbors. Over a period of time if we are not satisfied, expectations are not met, what do we do? We kick them to the curb. Wouldn't it be feasible to put as much time and energy into building a relationship with self for the betterment of self? How often do we take the time to know ourselves? How often are we honest with ourselves?*

*Questions we should ask ourselves and really take the time to think about them are:*

*Who Am I?*

*What do I like?*

*Do I even like me?*

*How many times do we have a relationship with ourselves to interview and question our belief system and when the expectations, wants and desires are not met do we kick our belief system to the curb? Too often we place more value on others and what we want others to give and do for us than we place on us doing for ourselves. We work on others issues and circumstances harder than we work on our own. Putting time, energy and effort into others hopes and dreams. When we are curbed, we are wondering what* happened and we are left disappointed. If we can look at ourselves and see the value of strength, confidence, fulfillment and be happy in depth, our end will be greater than our beginning. Remember, we have the right and the opportunity to remove all negativity and lack in our lives and transition to that which is positive and bountiful. There are times when I journal, I write a letter vomiting my thoughts on paper. Sometimes thinking as soon as I write this it is going in the trash; no one can ever read this. Journaling is for your eyes only, unless you want to share it. So don't concern yourself with the grammar, style or spelling. Just write. You will find when you start to write it will start to flow. When you feel you don't have anyone to talk to – JOURNAL. Allow what is inside of you to come out. Things you never knew about yourself will be revealed. For me, journaling is a time of expression. To be expressive is an art. Putting my thoughts, feelings and emotions on paper. Releasing whatever it is I am feeling at the moment. Allowing myself to be expressive gives me the opportunity to reveal that which is within. My hurts, my pain, my anger, my disappointments, my anxiety, my frustration, my fears and my hates. Then I look at my position in whatever I have written and the cause of why I am feeling these emotions and asking where am I, what and how I can change these negative feelings to peace, joy, happiness and love. Remembering I am responsible for me and me only. I am responsible for my thoughts, beliefs and actions. My happiness is my responsibility. That is where my FAITH comes in; having a stronger belief in the one who created me and having the willingness to be open, pliable and moldable. At times I feel like I am in the ring, knocked down, but I get back up. Yes, I cry and I encourage myself, I affirm myself. There are times when quiet time may be a struggle especially when I don't think I am where I want to be or where I think I should be. Talk about PATIENCE. A quote I learned from a friend, "If you lick the ice cream long enough you eventually get to the cone." Savor the moment; it is for your benefit as well as ours. Give yourself credit for taking the small steps. Embrace and celebrate where you are at this moment. The person you are at this moment. Remember, it is a process. There is growth and development in the process. If you are not where you were and if you choose to move forward you are not going to be where you are or the person you are today. You are the person you are today because you kept moving. Yes, situations occur, things happen but you are *still here. You are able to choose what you would like to do next, even if you are in a situation. You can get through whatever it is. At times I converse with myself quietly or aloud. I affirm myself. Some of my affirmations are – I am wise, I am stronger, I am confident, I know more now of what I don't want and what I do want. I am loving me!!! I am loving the person I have become. I am empowered. I am all that and a bag of chips, Costco size. I believe our thoughts need to be more of what we are doing, what we can do than what we are not doing or what we cannot do. We cheat ourselves and in the long run we cheat others from experiencing the power and the person we are created to be. Another friend made a statement that has really stuck with me. So much so, I repeat it in my conversation with others. In the summer of 2008, I was encouraged to take vocal lessons by a professional singer/songwriter. She was going to be doing a workshop and at the end of the workshop there was going to be a concert. I decided to come out of the box, raise the bar and attend the vocal workshop. The vocal coach encouraged me to participate and so I did. A door was opened so I walked through. This was unexpected, new and fun. After completing the workshop there was a concert. At the end of the concert my* friend came to me and said, "You have these gifts, these skills and talents, you're robbing me and I want them." Jokingly I told her I could sing back up for her and she said no. She told me I needed to be out front, no longer in the back. From that conversation I know I am no longer welcome behind the scenes of life, it is time to take center stage. It is time to be the person I am created to be and live the life I am created to live. It is time to take the limits off. Walk boldly on my path, my journey. I now share that story when I am speaking to others. Somebody is waiting for that treasure that is in you. It is not just for you. It is for everyone. It is time to take center stage. There is creativity within you; there are gifts, skills and talents within you. Imagine yourself having a great need for something and you are waiting for the resource. The person who is your resource to help you cannot do so because they are behind the scenes. They have not gone through the process of self-development. They have no vision, no ambition so you continue to wait. They are sitting, idling. Just as you are waiting, the field is waiting for you.

*What gift are you keeping from us? So there you are waiting. It is like waiting for a bus that never comes. You are waiting for the prepared person available to help you with whatever you're believing. There are times when we know we have gifts, skills, talents, possessions, resources, etc., but we don't believe in ourselves enough to put them into action. We don't follow through. It is one thing to have knowledge; it is another to apply knowledge. Applying is action. You can sit on your treasure all day, every day. Until you realize and believe you have value and move forward to free your treasure, your treasure will remain in its casket, buried. A treasure is considered valuable. It is cherished, it is held dear, something adored, precious, a work of art, a masterpiece, one of a kind, a gem, one in a million. You are unique and what you have is unique.*

*Discovery is essential. Realize and believe your value. Take action and start to unlock your treasure of love, self-worth, peace, happiness, joy, prosperity and success. You have the keys within you to do so.*

**Stop cheating yourself and robbing others of what belongs to them.**

## INVENTORY

*How much time are you devoting to you? If none, can you make time, whether five minutes, 10 minutes, make some time each day for you?*

*When spending time with self are you journaling your thoughts, your process? If no, why?*

*How often do you date yourself? (Get dressed, take yourself out whether to a movie, a park, lunch, dinner, a quiet stroll with nature, etc. Be creative).*

*How often do you affirm yourself?*

*What are some of your affirmations?*

*What gifts, skills and talents have you discovered within you?*

*Are you using your gifts, skills and talents to help others? If no, what is keeping you from using them?*

*What steps are you taking to excavate towards discovering you, discovering your treasure?*

# REFLECTIONS

realized since I was a child I have volunteered my time helping others. Between my mother and myself I was always a part of some group or organization doing something. When I was in elementary school I was what was called a "safety" with a badge. I wore an orange sash, and a metal badge that was pinned to the sash. I was a "child cop" with a badge on school grounds. Fights, hall monitoring, disruptive behavior, which was minimal during that time, it was my duty to make sure things did not get out of control. My position was that I would report what the teachers and staff did not see. I was responsible for the safety of the students at the age of "ten." I was my brother's keeper even back then. In middle school I was what was called a 'candy striper' at the hospital in the city where I lived. Sometimes in the summer I would volunteer with the Girl Scouts. Not a fan of the woods but I made the most of it. An experience I cherish. I always looked at my volunteering as fun. Helping someone else. As I stated when I volunteered at the hospital my title was "candy striper." A red and white apron that tied on both sides with one pocket in the front that went over my clothes was *my uniform. The apron looked like a candy cane with red and white stripes running vertically. That represented service. During my time serving, I had the opportunity to meet and talk with the patients while transporting them. It was rewarding listening to their stories and just being there for them. I learned from the experience. I gained from it as well. That is something that cannot be taken away that I am able to continue to instill. Meeting and talking with the staff, learning the different departments and areas of the hospital. Being a "candy striper" gave me an opportunity to experience different fields and different people. In 1976 at the age of 11 (sixth grade) I walked for the March of dimes – 20 miles for the support and fight against birth defects. A twenty-mile walk that took all day. Part of that process was asking for sponsorship for a great cause. I was doing this by myself. I remember the hills, up and down, walking by myself, the people behind me and the people in front of me, the people I met along the way. I was determined and committed to finishing the 20 miles. Parts of the day I remember it raining. I also remember sitting on the step when I got home, just sitting, rubbing my feet. I did it! What an accomplishment. The next day school was absent. I was still recuperating. As I write this* section it brings back the memories, the laughs and the fun in service – the people, the growth, the exposure to something new and different. Remembering the joy and happiness of my past with delight. I believe those things I did at a young age helped me to figure out what I like and what I did not like. What I could do and what I did not want to do. It was volunteering, so whomever and whatever I did not like I could always leave and do something else. Volunteering provided me with valuable lessons, one being looking beyond myself and considering the lives of others. There have been times when I have also created, facilitated and organized groups and events because that is what I felt would benefit an individual, the community, men, women, children and other countries. Empowering and enriching the lives of others I realize has been my journey. I realize that continues to be my focus and journey. Too often we look at not wanting to take advantage of what is presented or available because we are not gaining financially or materially. I may not have gained financially but I gained in ways that are PRICELESS and will never be taken away from me. I believe the wisdom and knowledge gained has helped to mold and shape the person I am today. I believe although I did not gain then financially, the skills I have obtained will help me financially now. Part of my journey included working in corporate America and also for non-profit agencies. I have gained much from both. I have enhanced and gained skills; my vision has better clarity. In one position I worked, I was fired because of my care and concern for others. I realized at times by helping others I would end up getting in trouble for others. This one particular time I was fired one cousin said to me, "I keep telling you, you can't go into someone else's house and rearrange their furniture. You need to have your own." I thought you are absolutely right! From that moment on I aspired to have my own. That became my focus. Having my own so I could arrange and place my furniture wherever I wanted to place it and move it whenever I wanted to move it. Along with that would come responsibilities as well, but they would be mine. There was a process to go along with creating my own. A process I believe included my entire journey. During this process I kept thinking about the name I wanted for my business. In 2008, K L Ross Enterprises was birthed. How exciting! I finally did it. I took the action, the necessary steps to go downtown and register my business name. I was going to *do this but I was not sure of the name or what needed to be done. I parked in front of the building still unsure of the name. But I was there. Going to make it happen. No matter how much I said I was going to register my business name that is all it was, me going. It was not until I took action, got in my car, drove downtown, filled out the necessary paperwork and went through the process did it become reality. A few months later I was considering a name change for the business. I mentioned to a friend who shared his belief of what an enterprise represented. His beliefs of an enterprise were not what I expected, but it made me think. As I thought about his beliefs I also wondered how to change that belief that would be more positive and productive. People say I am analytical so that part of me was looking at the negative and thinking how I could turn it into a positive. Something meaningful and productive. I also wondered how many other people had a similar belief.*

*K L Ross Enter-priSes is the result. I did not change the name. I created another way of writing it, with a positive meaning behind it. It was a long process that I am grateful/thankful for. One morning in January 2009, a* little before 2:00 I woke up and could not go back to sleep. I started thinking, my mind started wandering. I got up to get my recorder; thinking if anything started coming to mind I needed to be able to record it. And so I did. I recorded for about two hours. Thinking and recording, recording and thinking. To the point I believe I finally got it. K L Ross Enter-priSes is me. It is me personified. I am my business. My business is me. Everything I represent, my character, my gifts, my skills, my passion, my love, my strength, my faith is my business. It is all of who I am. It represents all of what I stand for and have done for so long. Those areas I personally worked on and became stronger in is now K L Ross Enter-priSes. I birthed a mini me to grow up into a greater me. It is a lot of what I stand for and believe – my being, my character and personality enterprised. I remember many years ago praying to be able to impact lives, saying if I can impact one life that is my reward. Since then because of the person I have allowed myself to become I can say I have impacted many lives for generations and that is my reward. To not just offer love, forgiveness, peace, unselfishness but **be** love, forgiveness, peace and unselfishness.

*K L Ross Enter-priSes is devoted to helping empower individuals especially youth. Our mission is to provide education and bring awareness for effectual change. Empowering lives and creating leaders is the pinnacle for excellence in individuals, families, communities and the world.*

*K L Ross Enter-priSes is a reflection of my journey. It is the person I have allowed myself to become. It is the freedom, time, energy and effort I have committed to. I know who I am and what I want to do and believing to the best of my ability doing it well will make a difference in the rest of the world.*

*What individuals, groups and organizations have you been affiliated with that have broadened your insight about you?*

*What opportunities were presented to you where you were placed in a position to help others? Did you take advantage of those opportunities? If no, why?*

# REFLECTIONS

# "OPPORTUNITIES"

*"Sunrise emanates a natural aura of beauty and warmth. As you go throughout your day allow your aura to emanate the same."*

*arly one morning this came to me and I shared it with a friend as he was on his way to work. I thought of the character of the person and what I saw in him. Have you ever watched the sun rise? How often do we pay attention to the beauty of the sunrise or nature for that matter? Do we recognize the beauty that surrounds us? In our society we have become busy and at times miss the warmth and beauty that is around us. We have become consumed and life just passes us by. Opportunities present themselves every day. Each day we wake up with the ability to breathe, we are given another opportunity to take advantage of possibilities. We can create success and promote advancement. We can choose to take advantage of the opportunities presented or we can choose to ignore them and continue to be where we don't want to be.*

*In 2003, I had to make a major decision because of where I was at that stage in my life. I needed to go to work but was unsure of the profession. I had worked in the technical field for fifteen plus years and wanted to change careers. I went through the interview process with myself. What do I want to do? What do I like to do? I knew I liked helping people. I had served communities for years as a volunteer. I enjoyed it and it provided a sense of pride and joy to know I could give my time, energy and effort to make a difference in the lives of others. I had served on various committees and organizations as president, secretary, treasure and committee member. I had created groups for women and children facilitating workshops and mentoring. It was who I was. It was part of me. It was December 2003 and I decided I was going to go to college, but for what? I was not 100% sure but decided I was going. I had attended technical school and school for spiritual counseling but now to think about going to college. Now to go through the process of college choice and major. Was there fear? Absolutely!*

*Here I was about 40 years of age entering into a culture as a non-traditional student. Not sure what to expect, or how I would do or handle it. One thing I did know was I needed to make a move. Time was passing and me sitting and thinking about doing it was not producing anything tangible. I started making phone calls, had several interviews and felt overwhelmed. I was in a time crunch because the next semester was about to start. I remember calling one college asking for admissions and ended up speaking with a person in the cafeteria. We had a conversation about what I wanted to do, what I was experiencing going through the process, and this person became the PR person for the college. After her commercial she said to me, "You better come here." I will never forget her. It is because of her belief in the college she was representing and her encouragement that I chose to attend Delaware Technical & Community College. That opportunity proved to be the life change I needed at the time and I am ever so grateful for the phone mix up. I had transitioned. The happenings that occurred to get me into the program, that was my miracle. Opportunities may present themselves in events, people, places or things. I look at the way opportunities are presented as a connection to my destination.*

*There are times when we are presented with an invitation and without any thought we immediately say no. Continue to do that and the time will add up and before you know it you are older wondering because you wandered. It is a decision we make. How often do we pray for our lives to be better or an opportunity or better health? How often have we said no and possibly turned down an invitation for an opportunity? Can you think of a time when opportunity for education and awareness for better health and a better life were presented? I have learned how opportunities have become the catalyst for helping me reach my pinnacle. I am open and willing to learn, gain wisdom, and meet new people that can impart wisdom to me. I have opened my closed mind to receive the daily directions for my journey. I believe I am the type of person who is open and willing. That makes it that much easier to fulfill my dream/vision. I am a summation of all my opportunities. Some have been positive ones, some negative, but I have gained something from each and every one of them. I realize there are times when I push forward because I am anxious to birth my treasure. For me doors have closed and new ones opened. I am thankful and grateful for the closed ones. I reflect on the lesson and cross the threshold of the new ones. Moving forward with expectation, commitment and motivation. When a door is opened the light is not always on. There are times when there is darkness, no direction. That is where*

FAITH in your CREATOR and believing in the person you are created to be will bring light to the dark. I would like to share part of a paper I wrote after completing my internship in Ghana, West Africa.

"Three years ago I was faced with a challenge. I was confronted with having to make a decision regarding the next step in my life. Having to make such a decision was a difficult one. I was recently divorced and unemployed. What was I going to do? What did I want to do? Those were some of the questions but I did not have all the answers. I was giving up what society would call security to become independent. There was no crystal ball and I was facing the unknown. I could have looked at my situation as an overwhelming challenge or an opportunity. I was 39 years young with no guarantee about the choice I was about to make. Emotionally, physically, spiritually, socially and intellectually I was being challenged. I had expectations but I was not sure how to fulfill those expectations. College had been a thought in my mind. Although I felt and believed returning to the classroom to further my education would be most beneficial, the thought of that was scary. The idea of being in college was intimidating. My perception and expectations preceded my confidence. This was a time to grow in FAITH. I decided to take the challenge, stand on my faith and trust and depend on my CREATOR for the outcome. This was going to be a NEW BEGINNING."

In life there are times of difficulty but it is our attitude and response that causes us to be victims or victors. I was on a journey to be victorious and being a part of the curriculum of Delaware Technical & community College has been part of that journey. Delaware Tech has played an integral part in the person I am and the choices I make today. It has afforded me the opportunity to mature, grow and learn the person I am. I learned my strengths, weaknesses and boundaries. It has proven to be the impetus I needed. Being a Human Services student, I learned the importance of working on self before being able to help someone else go through the process of change. There were areas that I needed to apply what I was learning and I am thankful for the process of change. Being a human services student I am thankful for my process of change. Being a human services student I am thankful for what the book and the classroom experience were able to provide me, but I am also grateful for the field experience. Being able to apply what was learned was essential in my personal growth as well as my respect and understanding of others. My depth of compassion and desire to help others grew, especially for women and children. Reviewing my journal entry from my first directed practice, this is what I wrote:

"Today was my directed practice interview. I was excited about starting the process and anxious about where I would be doing my internship. I was asked, 'What do you want to be when you grow up?' I hesitated because I was not sure. I felt unsure because my interest had changed and at this time I cannot say for sure what I want to do. But I know I want to help others."

Because the field of human services is a broad field, I had not pin pointed exactly what I wanted to do. I had ideas but nothing definite. I realized what I believed I wanted to do when I started the process and where I was now had changed. I found that as I was going through the process, working on my self-development, becoming more aware of self, I was becoming more important to me. College was not intimidating to me anymore. I was enjoying the process. Personal areas were being worked on and I could see growth. I believed my personal work was important to promote my overall well-being and eventually the well-being of others. A month after my first directed practice interview, I started interviewing with agencies to find my fit. My confidence with interviewing had improved. My journal entries reflect that. In my entries I referenced my levels of comfort without being anxious. This was growth. My choice in the field of human services was to work with the female population. Fit. August 2004 I found my fit. I chose to do my internship at an agency that serviced the homeless and impoverished. My first day at the agency this is what I wrote:

"Today was my first day. I was able to meet some of the women who use the services. I wish I could do more to help. Today I learned the phones, the logs and sat in on my first intake with staff. It was emotional, but encouraging that help is available to those who seek help."

The agency broadened my views and changed my perception regarding people in poverty. It helped me to understand what I learned at Del Tech and be able to use my skills in areas that I developed to help and encourage the women at the agency. Not to look at the women as less but as women with potential. I could possibly impact and help empower women to become productive citizens in today's society. To respect them where they are in life and help them with their physical, intellectual, emotional, social and spiritual needs. My first directed practice gave me a deeper insight into the world of homelessness, drugs, alcohol, abuse, being imprisoned and a woman's motivation to change. To help women go through the process of change by duplicating what was given to me made me appreciate more the need to work on myself. I understand the importance to a greater degree now. In my first summary I expressed being able to empathize with the clients, respecting them for who they are and not judging them for the situations they are in. Being able to sit, listen and talk to them helped my ability to communicate effectively with not only the clients but socially as well. I journaled at the end of my first summary how my overall experience had been enlightening, rewarding, educational and emotional and I was thankful for the process and looked forward to the continued growth and experience. Another entry that has helped me was when I talked about my wanting to make things better for the women. I knew they were trying and I wanted to make things easier for them. My feedback was,

"How about enabling them to make things better for themselves." That was EMPOWERING for me. Because of my desire to help others, I need not become overwhelmed with putting too much of me in their work but empowering them to do their own work. Working at the agency helped me to mature in dealing with my emotions. In my final summary journal entry I wrote:

"It's hard to believe I am done. Time has passed quickly. I remember the beginning being nervous about the hours, the seminar and expectations. Now I can ask, 'What was I nervous about?' It all worked out. The changes that occurred with me, the growth with communicating with others, being able to be objective with the clients, empathizing with them, learning skills relating to the field of human services. I became educated about another culture. The women educated me about addictions, prisons, street life, struggles, family, life, death, pain and hurt. This was from the women's frame of reference. Before that, I could only relate to what I had heard from others or seen on television. My time with the women enlightened me to another world outside of my own. I also stated, 'I respect the women for who they are, where they

have been and the drive to make a better life for themselves.'
I ended my summary with, 'I would like to continue by
volunteering my time, to continue in the process of helping
and impacting other's lives in a positive way, continuing
my journey in the helping profession."

My first internship challenged me to work on myself and
learn skills to work in this healing field. After completing
my time, I was able to use the skills I learned and apply
them in my personal life. I was maturing socially,
emotionally, spiritually and intellectually; becoming more
aware of working on my whole being. I was becoming more
knowledgeable and understanding of how each area is a
connection to the total well-being. My awareness and my
willingness to change became evident in my journal
entries. My second directed practice was a life changing,
empowering experience. The opportunity to implement
and organize my internship in Ghana, West Africa, caused
me to go beyond what I ever expected. Reflecting back to
when I first started at Del Tech, all that has happened goes
beyond what I could have ever imagined. Facing the
unknown to NOW the known, I am pleased and grateful
that I stood on FAITH and took the challenge. Going

through the process proved to be essential in impacting not only my life but also the lives of the men, women and children in Ghana. Organizing my second directed practice caused me to come out of my comfort zone and the box. It is still giving me an opportunity to work on myself. I believe working on me will be an ongoing process. Being able to network and express my views, wants and needs allowed me to observe and know the person I am capable of being. What I have been able to accomplish was not just education as far as academics but also education on a personal level. I have been able to establish relationships, aid in problem solving, communicate effectively, empathize with others, understand the developmental stages, set goals, work effectively on a team, plan programs and activities and continue to evaluate the areas of personal growth and awareness of a need for continued learning. In the beginning, I mentioned my growing in faith and dependence on my CREATOR for the outcome. On May 28th I journaled:

I am grateful and thankful for where I am spiritually at this time. I have become more confident in my being. This process has brought maturity with it."

*I also noticed in some of my entries the need to take time for me. There were moments I journaled my taking physical and mental breaks, relaxing and unwinding. Knowing the importance of taking care of the total being I realized at moments the importance of becoming more aware of my limitations and boundaries and being comfortable with saying "no." Organizing my second internship brought moments of frustration and difficulty, but it was mastered by motivation and purpose.*

*My experience in the Human Services curriculum at Del Tech has created an opportunity and a willingness to evaluate, learn and develop the necessary skills to grow and mature as an individual and then contribute to the lives of others. I have learned to mature physically, intellectually, emotionally, socially, and spiritually. I believe in the process and I look forward to the continued growth and the opportunity to help others "**trust the process**."*

*My time at Delaware Tech has proven to be a life changing experience. I have had access and opportunity to experience other cultures and build international relationships. I was part of the first group of students who participated in the study abroad program to Turkey. From there a door was opened and I was also given the opportunity to implement and coordinate my Human Services internship to Ghana, West Africa where I lived for two months. My focus now is to continue to help others nationally as well as internationally. My time at Delaware Tech has been a journey for learning and helping others.*

*Because of my service in Ghana, West Africa here is a letter I would like to share. A letter from a father who I was able to find sponsorship for his children to attend school. This letter he wrote:*

*"Dear Brethren,*

*I have two (2) happy days in my life. The first is the day I received Jesus as my Lord and personal savior. It was joy in my home and wish I could sleep in the church building overnight. The second was this January when Madam Karen Ross told me about the sponsorship from you to some of my children. After the discussion, I went to my room and broke down in tears and worshiped the Lord out of joy. Please allow me and my family to say thank you and GOD BLESS YOU. God should repeat all the miracles and blessings that have happened in your life. Amen. For now, the children you have adopted are for you. May GOD join their spirit to your spirit that you may feel their presence in your hearts and homes.  Amen*

*Greetings from Ghana and my family.*

*Thank you once again."*

# REFLECTIONS

# "TURKEY"

*A*n opportunity to study abroad in Turkey presented itself in 2005. The college had organized the first time ever study abroad program. I had not thought about traveling abroad but evidently one of my instructors thought and believed enough for me. One of my English instructors saw me in the hall one day and mentioned the trip and how she thought of me and felt I should apply. When she mentioned it I said ok and let it go. It came up again when another instructor mentioned it to me and then one day I was walking and I saw the flyer posted in the hallway. This was a social science class earning three credits while experiencing a different culture. They were offering four scholarships to selected students. Enrollment was limited to 16 students and all participants would enroll in Honors Sociology. The college had formed a partnership with two other colleges here in the States and co-sponsored with universities in Turkey. There was a selection criteria which included a pre-acceptance interview with the international education selection committee. I applied. I went through the interviewing process. On April 7, 2005 a letter saying, "Pack your bags!

*Congratulations you have been selected to participate in the study abroad program to turkey, June 2-18, 2005. Your letter of interest, instructor recommendation, and the results of your interview reveal your interest in learning about a new culture first-hand. It also stated the President of the college was so impressed with all the student letters of interest and teacher recommendations that he is going to provide an additional $1,000 stipend." Okay! Talk about excitement, surprise, shock, coming out of your comfort zone and other emotions all at once. I was chosen to be one of the pioneers of the first time ever study abroad program. This was going to be a 16 – day international trip to Istanbul, Ankara, Cappadocia and other parts of Turkey. This was also going to be a ten-hour flight. My farthest trip had been to Freeport, Bahamas, twice. I would like to share my letter of interest for wanting to study in Turkey:*

*"An opportunity to study abroad in the Republic of Turkey would allow me to experience a culture outside of my own. We live in a culture that is diverse and at times because of a lack of understanding can cause conflict and confusion. To live, learn and experience a diverse culture would not only be exciting but would enlighten and broaden my*

understanding of a society where traditions and norms would be unfamiliar and strange to me. As a Human Services major, to study the sociological aspect of Turkey, would be rewarding personally and educationally. The opportunity will challenge me to be open to beliefs of others. In the field of Human Services it is essential to understand the cultural beliefs of others to be able to provide assistance to them. It is imperative to be open to the diversity of others and understand every part of their being - spiritually, physically, psychologically and emotionally. My desire and goal is to help others in a society that is ever changing to become the person they can be. To be able to encourage and offer myself as a vessel to help others. It would be exciting to visit Istanbul, tour the various religious sites, museums and other points of interest, while studying such topics as Art & Religion, Gender, race and age. Again the opportunity to travel and study abroad in Turkey would be enlightening, enriching and rewarding in helping me to broaden my spectrum of another culture that is unfamiliar to me. Not just to hear or read about the beauty and history of this country but to experience it firsthand would be an honor. To receive a scholarship towards this venture would help make this a reality. It would afford me the chance to become educated in my field while allowing me the chance to grow as a women and an individual and later being able to reach back and help someone else."

Yes, I was chosen to be part of the pioneer group but this was truly going to be about studying. A condensed study. We had a meeting before leaving to get insight about what was expected. One insight was we were expected to journal everyday while we were there in addition to two days before leaving and one week after returning back to the states. It was also made known we would be moving around a lot and there would be a lot of walking. I also met my roommate who happened to be a Delaware Tech student.

I started journaling two days before departure and reading my journal now about what I wrote then showed feelings of excitement. Excitement for the unknown. How about that? No fear just excited. Not even feelings about the ten-hour flight. The last line of my journal entry read, "Being open-minded, ready to receive."

*Sharing My Journal:*

**June 3, 2005** *we arrived in Istanbul. The ten-hour flight was not bad. There is a big difference between being used to, at the most, two-hour flights and a full ten-hour flight. Once we arrived at the airport I noticed cultural differences. Ethnocentrism had set in. Evaluating other people and cultures according to the standards of one's own culture. This was going to be a life changing experience."*

*Turkey for me was just that, life changing. It was humbling, enlightening, personal development as well as academic. The biggest was the personal development. Living and experiencing a culture outside of the one I am in each and every day. The language, the country, the history, the people, the food. The places we visited were beautiful. The people we connected with were warm and welcoming. My first few minutes in Turkey I was already getting a lesson in the cultural differences and the need to respect them. Once getting to the hotel, getting our rooms and settling for a few, we took off running with a full busy day. What a beautiful place. The buildings, the scenery. Breakfast was different. It consisted of a hard-boiled egg, cucumber slices, sliced tomatoes, olives, cheese and watermelon slices. Also bread and tea which they call "chai. "Our adventure started after breakfast. We walked and climbed the hills and streets. Thigh burning hills. Breathtaking hills. Need water at the top hills. We visited the Topkapi Palace and Harem. The palace was beautiful. A lot of history. It was breathtaking. To see the beauty and think how it came to be was interesting to me. The planning, the work, materials, etc. The experience on our second day was an awe experience as well. Visiting the palace, enjoying the beauty and history made me think how much we are missing in the U.S. A difference I noticed was the affection shown for each other while walking down the street. Women walk arm in arm, men walk arm in arm and the children walk arm in arm. A difference from our culture.*

**Saturday, June 4, 2005** *my final comments entered into my journal was, "Today was FANTABULOUS."*

*One thing I repeat over and over again is the beauty in the architecture in Turkey. The attention to detail, the colors and the materials. I continued to be in awe thinking about the process and creativity of such beauty. I journaled how I could stand in one place all day and take in the beauty. I* was amazed. Words could not express my thoughts and feelings about what I as seeing. We also visited the underground cisterns, the blue Mosque, the Bath House which is now a carpet store. One of the days I state how friendships had been formed, experiencing so much of another country/culture. What an exciting day. Truly enriched. The day we left Istanbul we caught a ferry to the "Big Island" part of the Princess Islands. Later we would be taking a sleeper train to Ankara. I had never experienced a sleeper train until now. The morning I woke up on the train – first time ever. I sat in my space on the train writing, looking out the window and admiring the view. We had used just about every mode of transportation for this trip. Especially the feet. As I looked at the land I thought about creation. How GOD created all of what I was looking at. It was amazing to me. It made me appreciate what had been created even more. It took me to another level in life. Helping me grow. Helping me to become better to help others. My desire to help others, to encourage others comes from my ability to first encourage myself, work on myself first. I am work in continuous progress. I see this not only as an educational opportunity but an opportunity to encourage man, woman and child to *persevere. That there is so much more to life. To be forever learning. Life is a lesson. There is homework, there are tests and whether we feel like it or not, continue. Use life as a stepping stone to something much greater. The opportunity is there. But you must have a vision. You have to see past what is in front of you and the moment. Dream bigger. I thank my HEAVENLY FATHER for the opportunity and experience so that I might be able to help someone else. I believe that is what GOD wants us to do. Help those who are in need of help. I believe GOD places people in our lives at a moment when we each need help. So I need to be ready. I need to be at peace. Peace within myself, strong and confident in who I am and sure of my ability to help others. So many other people will benefit from this trip. Not just me!!!*

*The hospitality in Ankara, wonderful! The day we visited Ankara University Technical School they provided us with breakfast, lunch and gave us a tour of the grounds and a lecture. We were also able to visit the teacher's homes. We were their guests. The reception in Turkey has been wonderful.*

*Although we had been very busy on our trip I was thankful. I was seeing things I could never have imagined. The people, places and the fame. People treating us like celebrities. I don't get this at home. I was spoiled in less than a week. I thought, this is going to end. Back to reality. Some of the places we had traveled in ten days were Istanbul, Ankara, Cankiri, Kastomuno, Avanos, Urgup, Neshehir, Derin Kuyu, Aksaray, Tuz Golu – third largest salt lake and Golbasi. Wow!!! We have really covered some ground in ten days.*

**Tuesday, June 14, 2005** *part of my journal entry was as follows: Breakfast then to the U.S. Embassy. How exciting to actually go inside and learn what actually goes on there. I learned a lot about the activity of an embassy. More than I knew before going in. It has broadened my options as far as careers. I have to do more research. I could have stayed longer. I went back to the dorm wanting to wash clothes. There's that language barrier again. I did receive help from a student after several minutes of trying to communicate with the front desk. The student was a welcoming sight. She was really helpful. She wants to be a lawyer and would like to come to the U.S. It is interesting how some people in* the U.S. want to leave and people from other countries are trying to get there. Dinner tonight was pizza. Another educational, fulfilling, interesting day. Also presented to the staff, "What can we as students in America do to help students here in Turkey? I would really like to do something to help them. I presented doing a book drive for the libraries. Something I will work on upon returning to the U.S.

**Thursday, June16, 2005** *we are winding down. Time went quick - 16 days. Time flies when you are having fun. I have met so many people, experienced so much now it's about to end. I am somewhat sad about leaving. I am on the fence about returning to the U.S. I love the beauty here. To sit and look out and take in the beauty of this country. I wish I could bottle it and take it with me. Istanbul University. We were able to tour and meet with the President. Sit in the Senate room and share our experience and thoughts. We had chai and cookies. Preparing to return to Istanbul. Packing again. Leaving acquaintances and places that became part of us the short time we were in Ankara. Until next time!!! Off to the sleeper train.*

**Friday, June 17, 2005** *back in Istanbul. A familiar place. This is where we started. A different hotel though. The Best Western. American breakfast buffet. More Americanized facility. The view at breakfast was breathtaking. Looking out at the water,*

*the view of Istanbul. Today is our free day. Our time. We went to the Bazaar. We ventured out to the bazaars not too far from the hotel. We caught the train. Our last dinner in Turkey as a group. We talked about our experiences, laughed about some of our experiences. We said goodbye to two very helpful, pleasant, thoughtful guides. I will miss them. I appreciated all that they have done to make this experience an educational, enlightening life changing one. To all those that helped and became a part of this journey I am truly grateful.*

**Saturday, June 18, 2005** *the party is over!!! It has ended. 16 days. Wow!! My life has truly been affected by the last 16 days. Relationships formed. Experiencing the unknown. So much to share. Still so many questions. So much more I want to do now. More traveling, seeing more and learning a different language. It feels different as far as* *returning home. I am not as excited as I should be. I believe I should be more excited than I am. I don't mind returning. I am returning to what's familiar. I am being placed back into my element. What I consider normal??? The plane ride was not bad at all. I slept. At one point I found myself saying "thank you" in Turkish to an American flight attendant. He did not respond. That isn't going to be fun anymore. Again back to the norm. Say goodbye for now to the group. Some cried. We hugged, exchanged information then departed. It feels weird being back. I thank GOD for the trip there, during and back. Fantabulous!!! Wonderful!!! Life Changing!! I am a new improved Karen.*

**Monday, June 20, 2005** *I had thoughts of Turkey all day. The fun, the adventure, the people, the group, Delaware Tech and staff. Also thought about how much I want my life to change because of it. Reevaluating my beliefs, values and what I believe is right. My behavior, my attitudes. Where do I begin? One thing I saw being in Turkey is the value placed on family. Family taking care of each other. Always being there. To be able to have family, have a good time, laugh and talk is a beautiful thing. Being able to* *count on family. A community. We learned in Turkey the value placed on family as a child.*

*The importance of family growing up before secondary education. How family sets the stage. That is so true. Family influences affect so much of who we are later in life.*

*After returning from Turkey the question was, "What can we, as students in the United Sates, do to help students in Turkey?" The commitment I made to myself to help students was on my agenda. At the time I was President of Sigma Kappa Delta National English Honor Society and a member of Phi Theta Kappa International Honor Society. The word went out. With the help of members, students, staff and the President of the college in partnership with another college, we were able to collect over 1,000 textbooks from all Delaware Tech campuses throughout Delaware at the end of the semester. We were also able to collect about 50 computers. Talk about TEAMWORK!!!*

# REFLECTIONS

# "AFRICA"

*Welcome to the Spirit of Africa.*

*Africa often referred to as the motherland; rich with history yet her story seems irrelevant.*

*A culture of beliefs and values, music and dance dating back to the beginning of civilization.*

*Ancestors living the abundance and beauty of such a great continent.*

*A continent rich with natural resources but now lacking in power.*

*Our native land, crying out to be remembered.*

*Our motherland, with wealth in her bosom waiting, crying for her children to unite and partake of the vision, to partake of what lies within from the beginning.*

*Africa a culture where music originated.*

*The sounds, the dance continuing today prayerfully never to be forgotten.*

*To be passed on from generation to generation.*

*Remember your heritage, remember your ancestors.*

*I give you "a touch of culture."*

n July 2006, I had the opportunity to travel to Ghana, West Africa where I actually lived for two months. After our trip to Turkey, we were questioned by college staff about our adventure and goals. My response was, "I would like to do my second internship abroad." The response was whatever we can do to help let us know. That response came unexpectedly. I was then asked, "Where would you like to go?" Did not have a clue because I was not prepared for either response. After getting over the shock, it took a moment. I considered Africa. Next I had to consider and get verification from the Human Services department. The department chair and my advisor had to give permission as well. Things needed to be in place during my time in Africa. Arrangements had to be made with my advisor, there were guidelines I had to follow. It is one thing to follow guidelines locally, but when you are in another country and things are not in place it is another ball game. That was a process to trust. I had to have access to the internet, a phone, because the same directed practice guidelines that were in place had to be followed in Africa. I had to journal everyday for two months. I had to phone them to let them know my progress and that I was ok. During the summer there are no internships for Human Services. This would be an exception. The staffing is limited, but my advisor made an exception. This had not been done before so this was new for all. As I continued to think about it and everything that would have to be done I decided I wanted to implement, organize and raise funds on my own with no financial assistance from the college. My purpose was not only to experience a culture outside of the one I lived every day, but to also be self-sufficient and be the example that this can be done without financial support from the school. Ten months of preparation, perseverance, motivation and the "I can do this" mind, it was an extraordinary task. "I can do this" because "I did do this" and I am so glad I did not give up or think and believe that I could not do it. The opportunity I would have missed would have been much more disheartening not only for me but the people and lives I was able to be a part of during my stay. There are letters that reference my treasure of love, compassion, selflessness. How inspiring, how encouraging to know others see and reap the gifts that have been part of me from birth. To witness the joy and happiness is unexplainable. I watched in amazement. Something as small as a pencil, a book, things we take for granted they accept, cherish and *celebrate. They saw value in the smallest things and danced for receiving the simplest things. The owner of the school cried and said this was the first time in three years since they opened that anyone had given them anything. She said, "You are an angel." I was numb. I just watched and listened. One of the letters stated how the head teacher with tears of joy running down her cheeks shouted, "Jesus! We have never seen such a thing before in this camp." The purpose of my internship was to allow me to be in the population of the community I would be serving. To be the catalyst of hope. The resource of compassion. I remember watching the women and saying what these women and young girls have gone through in their country. Having to run for their lives not knowing if they were going to die, watching their loved ones die, leaving their families and not knowing if they would ever see them again. Some praying just for the opportunity to see their mother, their families again. To be in a world so big and wonder if that chance would ever come, that would be a miracle. My heart cringed at the thought. I tried to imagine what that would be like for me. As large as this world is to not know if I would ever see my sister, my family ever again. Asking and wondering what corner of the globe are they in?"*

*Wow! To see and work with the women that had suffered and to see them now committed motivated, caring, compassionate, I was in awe. No matter what they had been through they were getting the job done. Doing whatever was necessary to change their present situation. Talk about birthing a treasure. These women would come to training with their children tied to their backs, focused. They came prepared. The other gift I received from them was one of community, unity and family. They may not possess the material but they possess values. The importance of family and survival. How many of us can take that class and graduate? They saw me as a gift. They saw me as giving to them, but they gave me so much more. Where does it say only people that have material gain can impart riches? Never be blinded by the objects you see in front of you because they can be deceiving. Look inside and find the true value and worth before making a commitment to what looks promising. A letter written by one of my sponsors in Ghana, West Africa.*

*"I would like to express our candid impression about Karen Ross on her internship in Ghana. Her sterling demeanor in all her placements was indeed exemplary. Taking follow up*

*trips to all the places for programs, we receive remarks of her dedication and resolve. Karen tackled all the things she was involved in with commitment, diligence and concern for details. She was patient, kind and caring but firm. She was easy to get along with. Her sense of humor and humility made her get along with everyone she came in contact with. She was so adaptable that one could hardly realize that she was in a different environment. She tried to learn some of the local dialect. I can still hear the voice of Karen in my ears saying, "me dase" meaning thank you. This endeared her to all. Karen Ross exhibited commitment and love wherever she went. At the Liberian Refugee Camp, the school children always refused to go home after their lessons with Karen. I can picture the children in their numbers following her up to the school where we waited for her to get back home. At the orphanage Karen related to the children so well that the owner remarked, 'I wish you joined my workforce rather than going back to the U.S.' Touched by the level of poverty and the miserable plight of the needy, Karen quickly sold off her car even in the face of strong opposition and serious consequences. She rushed with us to town and purchased almost all what the school children needed to ensure a good foundation towards their better future. The school hitherto was a mere place of resting and playing for the children, because they did not have the needed learning materials. The Head-teacher with tears of joy running down her cheeks shouted, 'Jesus! We have never seen such a thing before in this camp.' Karen did not stop here. She left funds behind for the purchase of sewing machines, blender, materials for interior decoration, flour, sugar, etc., for the refugee vocational school with about 250 young girls and women. Their proprietress and the beneficiaries were indeed shocked beyond description. Karen Ross was indeed generosity and hard work personified! We all could not help but marvel at her kind-heartedness and commitment. We all pray that she comes back. Karen Ross of Delaware Technical and Community College came to Africa and offered a selfless and sacrificial internship. Kudos to Delaware College for such a product. We are yearning to receive more Delaware interns (Karens) in Ghana for that matter, Africa."*

*Delaware Technical & Community College you are part of me. To each and every one of you "me dase." The doors, the opportunities, the encouragement, unselfishness and the inspiration has proven to live up to the commercial that was given five years ago. Choosing the Human Services field was already who I was, it just magnified me and helped me to grow that much more. I will pass on to others what was given to me. Continue to serve and know that you do it well.*

*-Karen L. Ross*

# REFLECTIONS

# "FORGIVENESS"

## "You Inspire Me"

*At times we hold onto PAST issues and situations that occupy much of our time, energy and effort. We can't and don't grow because we are stifled. We suffocate our vision and our dreams by surrounding them with PAST hurts and pain. We have allowed bitterness and resentment to create stress and disease in our bodies. LET GO!!! BE FREE!!! There is NOTHING, ABSOLUTELY NOTHING we can do with PAST. We have actually made PAST a partner. We have allowed PAST to come in and take over. PAST is going to be the past. It is not going to change. We can either grow stronger from the experiences using PAST as a tool for building strength, confidence, and maturing us; or we can allow PAST to keep us from moving FORWARD to experience the love, peace, joy and happiness we deserve. We all can experience prosperity and success. It is whether you believe you deserve to experience prosperity and success. We all have choices to make. Some are harder than others. There are limited guarantees and many risks at the "University of Life."*

*Yes risks were taken, mistakes were made, but did you learn anything?*

*Can you turn and look at that lesson as an opportunity that excelled you?*

*Life is full of challenges. Challenges test your ability. Will you look at that challenge as inspiration or defeat? Graduate each challenge with hope. Forgive yourself and focus on this day. Close your eyes. Quiet your space, quiet your mind. Say to yourself, whatever I did, whatever happened in my PAST is done, it is gone. There is nothing I can do. The wrongs, the hurts, the pain I have experienced or the pain I have caused I cannot change. I apologize to myself, I apologize to those I have hurt and caused pain. To those that have hurt me, I FORGIVE you. Most importantly, I FORGIVE myself. Who I was in the past is not the person I am today. I am older, I am stronger, I am wiser. I am graduating from PAST. I affirm myself. I love me, I am beautiful and I am created for greatness. I am responsible for me, so right now, "It is all about me.*

*What are your beliefs about forgiveness?*

*What areas of your life do you need to work on as far as forgiveness? (Who, what, when, where)*

*Are there issues or people in your PAST that you are allowing to keep you from moving forward or causing you not to focus on you and being free?*

*Is it possible for you to forgive yourself and others? If no, why?*

*What would forgiving yourself and others mean to you?*

*Who or what inspires you or has inspired you? Focus on the inspiration within and the loving, positive inspiration of others.*

*Forgiveness is hard for many. Remember forgiving is not just for the other person(s), it is for you. Allow yourself to go through the steps, the process of forgiveness. See and feel greatness beyond people and situations. Free yourself!!!*

## REFLECTIONS

I volunteered with an organization working with adjudicated and pre-adjudicated youth. Once a month I would facilitate and do a talk with teen girls. During a session with them I passed out white roses. I chose white roses because they are symbolic of "NEW BEGINNINGS." For me it was regarding self-forgiveness and moving forward. As I was passing them out statements were made about how receiving the roses made them feel. One young lady expressed how that was the first time she had received flowers and she was going home to share them with her mother. I journaled my time with them and shared it with them several months later. This is what was written:

I thought about the white roses as being symbolic of new beginnings. That is where I am at this moment in my life. Always working on me, myself. Graduating to something new. New business, new relationships. Old things passed away all things become new. Stepping into a new phase. One never existing before. How inspiring. Divine Spirit, Divine Creator presenting things never experienced before. Asking for divine wisdom, creativity, guidance, believing He hears and knowing He wants the best for me. Stepping *into non-existence to make it existence. Speaking life, speaking change, empowered.*

*Again, sharing how one never received flowers before.*

*Flowers so plentiful and part of nature but failing to partake of what is given for dominion. Something so delicate and beautiful we miss the opportunity to embrace the delicacies of nature. To think about and appreciate what was spoken into existence in the beginning and considered "good." A garden of color, an array of unselfishness. Given to partake, enjoy. Out of love came new beginnings. Out of love comes inspiration. You inspire me. Be inspired.*

**Forgive yourself, forgive others.**

**Move forward to unlock your treasure.**

## INVENTORY

*What resources do you have, possess to help someone else?*

*How have you used those resources to help and inspire others?*

*What are your feelings when you use your gifts, skills and talents to inspire someone else?*

*Continue to take inventory of yourself to see what you are doing with your treasure to make a difference. Evaluate the needs of change and recognize the steps to take action to making a difference.*

*Whether a smile, a kind word or a nice gesture that is inspiration to many. We never know what someone is going through. We can speak life or speak death to someone. Be the difference in someone's life today and every day.*

# REFLECTIONS

# "WOMAN"

*A lady, gracious as can be*
*Her glide, her stride, mesmerizing.*
*As the breeze blows a field of flowers, her step, her stride*
*captivates the crowd around her.*
*Her presence, her aura, as the light of the sun blinding.*
*There is something about her.*
*She glides in to a room noticed by many.*
*Her smile, her voice, soothing to anyone present.*
*Who is this "Woman?" Nobody really knows.*
*All we know is, her presence speaks mounds about her character.*
*To see her, she exudes confidence, trust and loyalty.*
*She has a Godly presence about her*
*Who is she? No one really knows.*
*She appears to have it all together.*
*Her radiance, she is a true example of what a society,*
*a culture of girls should be.*
*It is not her clothes that personify who she is.*
*It is the look of beauty within that extinguishes the negative.*
*It is her glow that draws many.*
*Not a word.*
*The light that beams from her.*
*Who is this woman?*
*Does anybody know? Where does she come from?*
*Does anyone have a clue?*
*Does it really matter?*
*Just know she is a "WOMAN."*

How powerful!!!

Expression without words.

Just being.

Just presence.

A woman of grace and integrity.

**THAT IS A TREASURE.**

*"WOMAN" is a journal entry written during my time of volunteering with the teen girls. I at times would journal my sessions with them. This particular entry was from our discussion of being a woman, a lady. We referenced the "white roses" that were presented during one of my previous sessions with them talking about self-forgiveness, new beginnings, second chances.*

# REFLECTIONS

# "WHO AM I?"

*his book has shared some of my process and my having to "**trust the process**." It has not been easy but that which is worth accomplishing never is. There have been risks taken and challenges to face. To trust and go through the process has been a rewarding task. FAITH, confidence, strength, love and compassion are assets that came through investing time in **ME**. It was realizing that it needed to be about me first. Being and staying focused no matter what. Once building and birthing me, I can then help someone else. Dealing with self is never pleasant. Of course, it's easier to look at someone else and tell and show them their "stuff." The put offs of what has been developed, what I have been conditioned to, believing my thinking was correct creating lack not just financially but emotionally spiritually, and physically. It was not until I became aware, made the decision for change, became wiling and took the steps to make change, was I able to be used as that catalyst, the vessel to create change around me. I realized who I was. I could now stand strong in my beliefs about who I was and what I wanted to do. I was comfortable with the person in my space. I realized my potential. Now I am* able to share and pass on my lesson to encourage and inspire others. I share this because, as stated earlier, we know we need to change but we refuse to because of fear, hurt, pain, or ego, the list goes on and on and on. We hold on to the negative but realize when we do that we cheat first ourselves then others. We are responsible first for ourselves. Be at peace with yourself, love yourself, forgive yourself and allow the "**true you**" to experience the best life you cannot imagine. Birth and be the man, woman or child you are created to be. The choice is yours. Make that choice today. You will be the better because of it. I am the compilation of the past and present moving forward to my future. I LIVE MY TRUTH! I LIVE AUTHENTICALLY!

# INSPIRATION

*Expression is the process of making known your thoughts or feelings. Making known the hurts and pains, the disappointments and frustration within. Putting an emotion to words. Communication of what is within. Sharing your thoughts of feelings is an art that comes from within.*

*Whatever your dream is, whether it is going back to school, starting a business, singing, traveling the world, being proactive towards wellness, becoming the President, etc., research, do your homework. Do something that will move you that much closer to your dream. If you do nothing short term, the nothings equate to nothing long term. Connect to yourself and go through the process. Then connect to a team of responsible, committed, motivated, qualified people who can help you through the process. Go through and "**trust the process**." Learn as you go and you will be better for it. Not only your life will change but the lives of others will be impacted by your willingness to submit to the "POWER WITHIN."*

*Believe in yourself. Believe in yourself. Believe in yourself.*

*Did I say believe in yourself?*

*Because*

*I Believe in You!!!*

*"Birth Your Treasure Within"*

# REFLECTIONS

## "FRIEND"

*Friends are the beauty of a bond*
*A partnership of sharing*
*An alliance of caring*
*A common interest coupled with understanding*
*Love being the adhesive that holds it together*
*Never judging but discerning with wisdom*
*Never doubting but believing*
*Never discouraging but inspiring*
*Forever be inspiring, forever be love, forever be a friend*

*I became friends with a young lady during my study abroad program to Turkey. Since 2005 we have become friends and she has been influential in the manifestation of this book. She spoke this book into existence. There were times we would talk and she would say. "I am waiting for the book." My response would be, "Yeah, ok." Another time she would say it again and I would respond, "Sure, ok." Who knew four years later in 2009 I would be releasing my very first self – published book. There are times when other people can see your gift and speak life into your SPIRIT. No matter what I was going through she would say, "I am waiting for the book." She held fast and strong to that belief. She believed it for me. She believed even when I didn't. She saw my treasure and was one of the tools to unbury that which was within. Maegan Pittman, I say "Thank you" for seeing and believing through the years what I did not.*

*To another friend who encouraged me as well to write my story. I finally got in January 2009. Emilyn DeGannes I say, "Thank you."*

*To my baby sister Thisha Forney, thank you for at times being my big sister as well as friend. Thank you for sharing your life with me.*

*"THANK YOU" to everyone who has crossed my path along my journey. You have played an essential role in me birthing my treasure and being the "gem" I am today. The wisdom, strength, support and most importantly the LOVE I have received, helps me to share with others my value and help others realize theirs.*
*HERSTORY has been made.*

*To my friends/sisters Kimberly Jihad and Sharon Warren. We have shared so much. I thank you for being there through it all and allowing me to share my life with you.*

*To my dad's Tommie Lee Clark and Robert Lee Ross I say, "Thank you."*

*To my heritage, my ancestors, the Jacobs/Ray/McAllister family, thank you for your love, support, faith and wisdom.*

*Lastly and most importantly my CREATOR, my Spiritual Father, the one who shaped and molded me into this vessel to be used for His purpose. Thank you for the opportunity to serve and make a difference in the lives of others no matter the culture. Thank you for the unconditional love you have bestowed upon me. That which you have given to me I pass it on. I thank you for FAITH and STRENGTH to move FORWARD. Thank you for being my FATHER and FRIEND. "You said I could."*

*In the beginning heaven and earth were created and proclaimed "good."*

*Part of creation is the essence of flowers*

*Different shapes, sizes and color*

*Each and everyone unique and beautiful*

*Unique and beautiful in purpose*

*Unique and beautiful in presence*

*Unique and beautiful in strength*

*Unique and beautiful in character*

*Unique and beautiful in greatness*

*Unique and beautiful and proclaimed "good"*

*Celebrate the flower in you*

*The field is blessed*

# FATHER KNOWS BEST

*I know I can live*
*Because my father gave me life*
*I know I can shine*
*Because my father gave me light*
*I know I can harvest*
*Because my father planted the seed*
*I know I can win*
*Because my father is my coach*
*I know I can love and inspire*
*Because my father is love*
*I know I have faith*
*Because my father gives me hope*
*I know I am protected*
*Because my father covers me*
*I know I have strength*
*Because my father is strong*
*I know I can lead*
*Because my father is my mentor*
*My father is my hero*
*Because he said "I could"*

# WHAT IS YOUR TREASURE?

*Karen L Ross is "inspired to care and prepared to lead."*

*Karen's commitment for making a difference in the lives of others deems her an inspiration and a social activist in its own right.*

*Her vision, dedication, commitment and perseverance have earned honors and recognition in her course of studies, community and among peers.*

*Karen continues to mentor men, women and youth to create and flow in a mindset of worth and wellness.*
*She is making a universal difference.*

*Karen is a businesswoman, writer, self-published author, speaker, consultant, and mentor.*

**"Be Inspired, Be Inspiration"**

**Live to YOUR fullest and greatest potential!**

Made in the USA
Middletown, DE
09 September 2024